Drive your Motorhome Like a Pro

A complete guide to professional driving techniques for beginners to experienced drivers

LORRIN WALSH

Printed by Gorham Printing, U.S.A.

ISBN10: 0-9785788-0-5
ISBN13: 978-0-9785788-0-0

CONTENTS

v   Preface

vii Acknowledgments

ix Introduction

1   **Chapter 1 • Maneuvering Basics**
    Basic Mechanics of Turning
        Pivot Point
        Off-Tracking
        Tail Swing
        Setup

9   **Chapter 2 • Getting Ready**
    9   Pre-Trip Inspection
    12 Seat Position
    13 Setting Mirrors
    16 Overall Dimensions
    17 Securing the Coach

19 **Chapter 3 • Driving**
    19 Steering
    21 Reference Points
    23 Mirror: Friend or Foe?

24 Transmissions
25 Advisory Signs
25 Merging
26 Downtown
29 Backing
29 The Parking Lot
30 Adverse Weather

33 **Chapter 4 • The Art of Braking**
    34 Air Brake Systems
    36 The Braking Equation

39 **Chapter 5 • Mind Set**
    39 Perception Driving
    40 Principles of Smart Driving

47 **Chapter 6 • Homework**

49 **Chapter 7 • Closing**

51 **Appendix Data Worksheet**

53 **Order Page**

PREFACE

When most people were taught to drive they were just taught the hows and not the whys. Teaching the whys, or the mechanics, of driving gives people the tools and skills they can apply to any vehicle or situation.

I am not a big fan of additional licensing, but I do believe a person should have some form of additional training when he or she operates a vehicle that would require additional licensing if driven commercially. This book is intended to provide that training.

ACKNOWLEDGMENTS

I thank all my friends who persevered throughout my ramblings over the last few years and sat through practice seminars. I also thank Gray Line of Seattle® for teaching me what I thought I knew, but didn't.

I cannot continue without thanking my wife for her support in this venture.

INTRODUCTION

I know what your first questions are going to be. "Who is this guy, and how does he know this stuff?" We bought our first motorhome in 1975 after trading in our trailer. We are currently on our fifth motorhome.

I considered myself a skilled driver after this many years of motorhome experience, but then, a few years ago, I went to work for Gray Line of Seattle®. As I went through their training course I realized how much I didn't know and how much I knew but didn't understand.

When driving a larger vehicle, like a motor coach or motorhome, the larger size and weight make maneuvering that you routinely do in your car seem totally different.

Currently I am a Driver/Guide and an instructor for Gray Line of Seattle®. As an instructor I train people to drive motor coaches from 20′ up to the Prevost H5-60, 8½′ x 60′ x 13′, with steerable rear wheels. The standard coach used for training is 8½′ x 40′ (and no, we do not have dual controls. You can imagine the fun of taking someone through downtown Seattle for the first time). One of the things that I find when instructing is that the students know how to drive, but they generally don't understand the mechanics of driving. Gray Line of Seattle® has been in business since 1909, and the materials that I use as an instructor are the product of over ninety years of experience.

I have developed this book from three sources: my experience as an instructor, the *Washington State Commercial Vehicle Guide*, and my personal experience of over thirty years driving motorhomes. At this point I should note that this book is not sponsored by Gray Line of Seattle®, and it is not intended that this book teach you to be a commercial driver.

I had a student who had driven city and school busses. She was a good driver. In her previous training she had been taught how to make maneuvers, but not the technical aspects. She was taught things such as "turn when the curb reaches the second window post" but not *why* she needed to wait until the second window post to turn. I call this "reference point" driving. After two days on a skills' course, she came to me and said she had thought she knew how to drive, but now she realized she didn't.

After a while you will start making maneuvers based on reference points, which is not a bad thing. But because the reference points will be different for each vehicle, I believe in teaching the rules so you will understand why you need to do a specific action. An example would be that I could take just about anyone and explain how to drive a forty-foot motor coach through a slalom course with forty-foot spacing. I can tell you exactly where to have the cones in the mirrors to make the turns, but this information is useless for driving your own rig. By understanding the rules, you can apply them to anything you drive.

I have found that the information provided in this manual has proven to be as useful to the experienced driver as it has been to the novice.

CHAPTER 1

Maneuvering Basics

"You want me to put it where?"

I was watching an interview with an Indy 500 racecar driver several years ago and he said, "Anybody can drive an Indy car at 200 mph in a straight line; it is when you need to turn that the problems start."

I think that statement is very appropriate to driving a motorhome. When you bought your motorhome I'm sure the salesman said something like, "It's just like driving a car or an extended cab pickup." Well, it is and it is not! It may be just as comfortable, and basically they do drive the same, but the dynamics are much different. The best way I can explain driving a motorhome is that you are getting the same perspective as if you were sitting on the hood of your car as you drove down the road.

Technically, there are two types of drivers: personal and commercial. But in actuality there is a third, a "professional" driver. Most people think of a professional driver as one who gets paid to drive. But one of the definitions of a professional is a person who does something with great skill.

My goal is to provide you with the tools you can apply to help you become a professional driver. That means professionalism developed by the ongoing awareness of driving motor coaches, and the execution of unique driving techniques needed to become a safer and a more confident driver.

The bigger the coach the easier they are to drive down the road, but they present more challenges when you start to maneuver or stop. Some of the information I will provide, you may be doing already—if so, good! Some suggestions I have, you may question; however, please give them a fair chance. If I can leave you with one tidbit of knowledge that prevents one bump or scratch, then my time and yours has all been worth it.

I have heard many stories about tight situations that people have experienced. Most of the time, it is a lack of understanding of the dynamics of the coach that make it a "tight situation" to begin with.

To understand how to maneuver in tight quarters you need to know how to properly set up or prepare for the maneuver. You need to know where to place your pivot point based on how much your coach off-tracks and how much tail swing you have. When you know these factors, then you can establish how you want to set up. Okay, I know you are asking yourself, "What did he just say?"

I will start with some basic definitions:

The **pivot point** is defined as the fixed point on a vehicle at which the vehicle rotates around in a turn. On a two axle vehicle it is the center of the rear axle. This means that if an object, for example a tree, is located at the center of the rear axle or behind, you can turn toward the object and not hit it. If the object is ahead of the pivot point and you turn toward it, you *will* hit it.

Off-tracking is the difference between the path of the front wheels and the rear wheels, during the course of a turn.

Tail swing is the distance the body of the coach behind the pivot point moves in the opposite direction of the front when you turn.

Setup is how you position your rig to start a maneuver after taking all the above into consideration.

Okay, let's take a look at each one and see the effect it has on your maneuvering.

On most vehicles you will not be able to see the rear wheels, so you will need to establish some reference points to know where your pivot point is located when you are looking in your mirrors. Look at the rear wheels and identify a spot on the side of the coach that is in relation to the center of the rear wheels. Putting a cone or something on the pavement to mark the center of the wheel will help locate your pivot points initially when you are looking in the mirrors. An awning arm, compartment door edge, a light, anything at or slightly behind the center of the rear wheel, that you can see in your mirrors, will do. Be very careful about using lights. Some manufacturers are good and put the side lights at the pivot point, while others just put them anywhere, usually ahead of the pivot point. I have seen vehicles where they are even at different locations from one side to the other. This can make maneuvering at night more of a challenge.

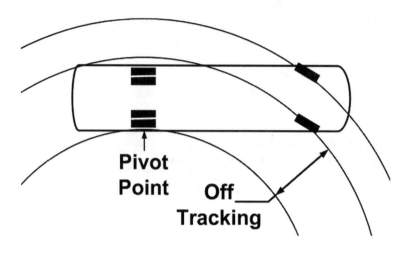

Off-tracking.

You really don't need to know how much your coach off-tracks, you just need to know what it is and how it affects the way your coach turns. What is beneficial is to establish what I call **turn offsets**. A turn offset is the distance that your coach will travel forward during a turn in relationship to how far you were away from an object when you started the turn. It basically shows you how your coach turns. Let's take a look at how you can establish this information and how to use it.

This is where you will need to do some homework. I have included a Data Worksheet in the appendix to record your findings. My suggestion is go to a large parking lot, like a mall, in the morning when traffic is light.

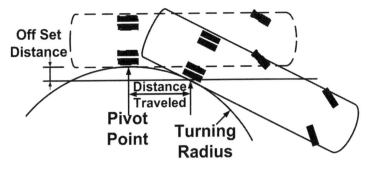

Off Set Distance

Distance Traveled

Pivot Point

Turning Radius

Turn offset.

To establish your turn offsets, park your coach parallel to a line one foot away. Then mark the line adjacent to your pivot point. Now, turn the wheels full lock, (as far as they will turn in the direction you want to go), in the direction of the line, and move forward until the pivot point you established on the coach intersects the line. Then, measure the distance that you have traveled from the starting mark that you put on the line to the pivot point. For my motorhome the distance traveled was seven feet.

It doesn't hurt to take these measurements turning both left and right. This gives you an opportunity to see what it looks like in the mirrors, and not all vehicles turn the same in both directions.

Repeat this exercise at two, three, and four feet from a parallel line. If you tow something it would be a good idea to take it with you when you try this, to see where the tow vehicle crosses the line. Then you know what to expect from it.

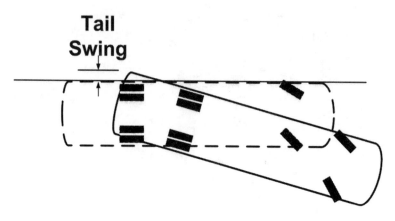

Tail Swing

Tail swing.

To establish what your tail swing is, stop your coach with the side of the coach along a straight line. Then, make a full lock turn away from the line and have someone measure the maximum swing as you turn. My personal coach has a tail swing of eighteen inches, but a coach I borrowed for some testing had thirty inches.

In general, a newer chassis will turn more sharply, which equates to more tail swing.

I always thought that tail swing damage would be the most common type of damage, but after talking to some service departments, I learned that they see tail swing damage as the second most common. The most common area damaged while driving is the upper right corner of the vehicle. This is caused from crowned roads and poles set close to the side of the roadway. You also need to be watchful to clear road signs.

After you have gathered your turn offset and tail swing information, you will know what you need to do to properly setup for a maneuver. The setup is the most important part of a maneuver.

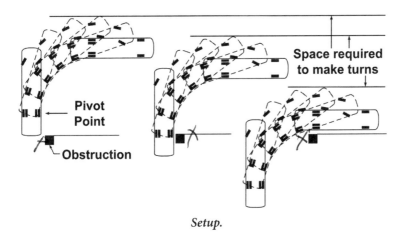

Setup.

If you look at the setup sketch examples you will see the same turn setup from three different starting positions. On the left you see the coach starting its turn when the rear is adjacent with the obstruction. The middle view shows the coach starting its turn when the obstruction is adjacent with the pivot point. As you can see, the overall space required to complete the turn is shortened by the length of the rear overhang. The turn on the right shows what can be done when the turn offset data is applied. By setting up further away from the obstruction and starting to turn earlier, you would be able to turn into a much smaller lane or opening. Also, by knowing your tail swing you know at least how far to be from a wall or other objects before you start your turn. In traffic you will need to allow space in the lane on the opposite side from the direction that you are turning, for your tail to swing into.

Something I need to stress here is don't force a turn. If there is not enough room to make the maneuver, stop and wait for traffic to clear to complete your turn. And if it doesn't look like there is enough room to make the maneuver, *don't do it.*

Remember the example I gave earlier that the perspective of driving a motorhome is like sitting on the hood of your car? Notice the path the front wheels take in the turn, and you are sitting ahead of them. Your car does the same thing, but you sit in the middle and don't notice it.

If you haven't realized it yet, what I am telling you is that you are actually "*Steering from the rear.*" It is what you do when driving anything, but it is not apparent until you drive a longer vehicle.

Drive smart: Maneuver with skill.

CHAPTER 2

Getting Ready

"Where do I start?"

Your motorhome, generally, is not driven at the same frequency as your car so there are some things that you should do before you start a trip.

Pre-Trip Inspection

As a commercial driver, I am required to perform an extensive list of inspections and document them on a Vehicle Inspection Report. There are all sorts of lists out there on what to check before starting. If you follow one of them, good for you. If you don't, I would recommend the following as a minimum:

1. Do a basic leak check. Are there any puddles or streams running under your coach?

2. Check basic fluid levels, oil and water.

3. Start the engine and check the instruments. Do you have oil pressure; is the electrical system charging? If the engine does not start right away it is better to let the engine crank for a while, (i.e., 30 seconds), rather than using short bursts of the starter. This is especially important for diesel engines. The highest battery draw is when you start to turn the engine over. Once you get the engine rolling, the starter draws a lot less current.

4. Check your tires. The best way is to use a pressure gauge, but at a minimum "thump" them. Use a steel bar or hardwood stick and hit the tread face of the tire, not the corner or side. This gives you the best indication. A properly inflated tire will have a ringing sound, while a flat tire just thuds. After a while you will even be able to tell when a tire's pressure is low. Periodically I will use a pressure gauge to ensure that the tires are at the manufacturer's recommended pressure for the load being carried.

Check the face of the tires to see how they are wearing. Are they cupping or scrubbing? That would indicate you may have an alignment problem. It is better to find out early that you have a problem before you ruin a tire.

If possible also check the lug nuts to see if any are loose. Ideally you would check the lug nut torque with a torque wrench. Checking the lug nuts by trying to turn each one by hand is a good basic check. If you see rust trails from any of the lugs, even if they are tight, have them checked, as it could indicate a problem.

Also don't forget to check your spare tire once in a while.

While I am on the subject of tires, let's talk about flats. If you have a flat outside dual tire, you can drive at slow speed for a reasonable distance to get to a safe location. If you have an inside dual flat, don't move the coach at all. A flat inside dual can damage the brake lines.

5. Check *all* your lights, including the four-way flashers.

6. Since you are walking around the coach anyway, checking tires and lights, it might be a good time to check:
   - Are the jacks up?
   - Is the antenna down?
   - Are all the compartment doors closed and latched?
   - Have you removed all the wheel covers and chocks?
   - Are all the services (power, water, cable) disconnected?
   - Are there any unusual sounds?

7. Don't forget to check the inside of your coach also.
   - Is everything stowed?
   - Refrigerator door latched?

When you stop during the day do a mid-trip inspection, a basic observation check. Walk around to check the tires and general conditions.

When I stop for a break I will take my tire thumper and walk around the coach and check the tires. I will also feel each tire with the back of my hand to check temperature. I have heard about people who recommend using infrared temperature sensors to measure tire temperatures. My response to that is, there is nothing wrong with doing it that way, and if you want to do that, knock yourself out, but don't "techno" yourself to death. When you stop and find one tire a few degrees warmer than another it may be nothing more than an uneven road surface that has put a little more load on one tire or the other. When driving on roads that have ruts from 18-wheelers your track width is slightly different so your tires get uneven loading, which will cause uneven temperatures. It could also be as simple as one side of the coach has been in the sun all day. Don't chase something that you can't do much about. The back of the hand will give you a good general indication of how things are doing. The back of the hand is more sensitive than the front, which has built up calluses over time that reduce sensitivity.

The bottom line when you are checking pressures and temperatures is, "The more accurate the measuring instrument, the more unobtainable the goal."

At the end of the day do a walk-around just like the pre-trip inspection. It is better to find a problem at the end of the day so you have time to take care of it, rather than in the morning when you are trying to get underway.

Seat Position

Positioning the seat properly is a subject that I think people really do not understand. The first thing is to use good posture—sit up straight, just like your mother told you to do!

If your seat has a height or tilt adjustment, position it so there is a slight space between the lower portion of your upper leg (just above the knee) and the seat. This space is helpful as it aids circulation. Reduced circulation in your legs can cause fatigue and cramps. If your seat has no height adjustment, consider raising the floor level by making a small platform.

For conventional pedals that hang down, having your heel on the floor is the proper position, but if you have full foot pedals, (ones that hinge on the floor), you need to be able to place your entire foot on the pedal. If you do not have the seat set properly your foot will only be partially on the pedal, and it will take several times more pressure to move the pedal. This reduces control and causes fatigue. An example of what can happen when drivers have only part of their foot on the pedal is that they tend to have difficulty maintaining a constant speed.

Don't worry if these seat adjustments make the top of the wheel unreachable. I will cover the proper way to steer a little later.

Setting Mirrors

Proper mirror setting is probably the most important part of getting ready. Approximately 30 percent of the hazards that you will encounter come from the rear, so getting the maximum viewing area from your mirrors is very critical.

If you have the type of mirrors that are fixed on the sides of your motorhome that's okay, just set them as detailed later in this chapter.

If you have the type of mirrors that stick out in front of your motorhome on long arms, you need to ensure that the inside edge of the mirror is flush with the side of the coach. In my observations, most motorhome mirrors of this type are not set correctly.

Stand in front of your coach and sight down the side. The inside of the mirror head should look like it is just touching the side of the coach. Having the mirror flush with the side of the coach gives you the best overall view. Some coaches taper in on the front and can give you a false setting so make sure you are looking down the side.

On the passenger side you should set the mirror flush with the outside of the awning arms. If the mirror is too far in or out, you are losing valuable viewing area.

On some coaches the driver's side mirror is located in such a way that when you have the mirror flush with the side of the coach, the corner post is in the way. If this condition exists, consider swinging the arm around to the back so the mirror is visible in the driver's side window. This is what is done on most motor coaches. This will also give you more room when maneuvering in tight places. You may have noticed that many of the newer coaches come with the driver's mirror mounted on a short arm on the driver's side.

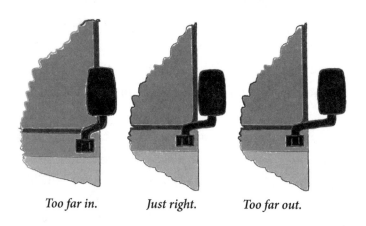

Too far in.   *Just right.*   *Too far out.*

If the mirror is too far in people will generally set the mirror looking straight back along the side of the coach. If you do this you lose viewing area to the outside. If you set them so you just see the front edge of the coach on the inside edge of the mirror, you are creating a blind spot alongside the coach.

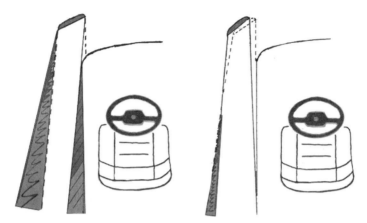

Shaded areas show lost viewing areas.

If the mirror is too far out and you set it so you can see the side of the coach, you are losing viewing area to the outside. The further out you have the mirror head, the more viewing area you lose.

The view is free—use it, do not waste it.

Set mirror looking level one-fourth the way down.

Adjust the flat part of the mirror so you can just see the side of your coach along the inside edge and so you are looking back level with the ground about one-fourth of the way from the top of the mirror. You really don't need to see a lot of sky, unless you are driving on a runway.

15

If the convex (a.k.a. "spot") mirrors are independently adjustable, set them the best you can so you can see out horizontally to the ground and alongside the coach. Most people do not use their convex mirrors for general driving because it is not easy to see any detail. You may not see the detail, but the fact that you are seeing a much larger area gives you an advantage.

Think of your spot mirrors as an early warning device. They give you warning of a developing situation around you in order for you to take needed action. It may take several seconds for what you see in your convex mirror to show up in the flat mirror, if it ever does. I will talk about what to do with that extra time later in the book. When set properly the convex mirrors should be used as much as the flat mirrors for general driving. Sometimes when training coach drivers we will cover up the flat mirrors to force them to learn how to drive using the spot mirrors. If you don't have independently adjustable convex mirrors, consider installing some. There are many types and kits available.

Overall Dimensions

It is a good idea to know the overall dimensions of your coach before you come to that low overpass and it is too late.

You should measure your hard and soft clearances as well as width. Hard clearance is the height of the tallest hard object on the roof, like the A/C or satellite dome. The soft clearance is the height of your antennas. This will help you make the decision to go under something at speed or to slow down.

One way to establish your heights is to find a level spot and get a laser level and a tape measure.

Measure your overall width, including mirrors and awnings. I think this is especially important with class C motorhomes. Many people buy these vehicles because they have a more comfortable feel in the cab. What they fail to remember is that they stick out as much as twelve inches on the sides and as much as five feet above your line of sight overhead to the top of the A/C.

"Why width?" you ask. You never know when it might be important to know. If you have ever been to the Black Hills of South Dakota there are several tunnels that you may or may not fit through, and you do not want to find out after you start through. I have walked through the tunnels and found many broken mirrors. People would unhook their trailers, but leave their towing mirrors on.

Use the Data Worksheet in the appendix to record your dimensions. It would also be handy to have the metric conversions, just in case. On my personal coach I have taken the dimensions I established and put them on a plaque attached to the dash.

Securing the Coach

It is very important that you have complete control of your vehicle at all times. The best time to take control is when you are starting or stopping. You should always have two means of control, the parking brake and the foot brake or the transmission and the foot brake.

When un-securing your coach, hold the foot brake, put the transmission in gear, and release the parking brake. Before starting to move make a full or 100 percent brake application to make sure your brakes have released. This will apply more to air brakes because some systems will require that more pressure be applied to release the brakes than was used when they were set. If you had your foot hard to the floor when you set the parking brake, you may have trouble getting the brakes to release.

When securing your coach, hold the foot brake with the minimum amount of pressure required to keep the coach from moving. Then apply the parking brake, shift into park or neutral if you do not have park, and release the foot brake, ensuring the coach does not move.

Drive smart: Know your coach.

CHAPTER 3

Driving

"Boy, this thing is big."

Now let's take the information I have given you and apply it to going down the road and other real-life situations. There are many techniques that can help you become a safer, more confident driver. How to steer using reference points; how to drive in congested traffic like downtown; how to use your transmission; and merging in traffic are just some of the things that I cover in this chapter.

Steering

The steering wheel position on motorhomes is different from that on cars. The wheel is usually larger and set flatter, especially on the pushers, which means you need to use a different technique to steer than you are accustomed to. It is called **shuffle steering**. Relax the upper portion of your arms along your side and extend your lower arms straight out to where they touch the wheel. Don't reach for the top or outer edge.

Your grip needs to be soft, like driving with eggs in your

hands. This gives you much better control and also reduces fatigue. You turn by shuffling the wheel through your hands so that you always have both hands on the wheel. Never let it "freewheel" when coming out of a corner. You can practice the shuffle-steering technique when driving your car. If you feel as if you can't keep up with the steering wheel when shuffle steering, then slow down, you are probably taking the corner too fast anyway.

When you reach out in the 10 and 2 o'clock position, you do not have good leverage and your arms will get tired faster. The best way I can explain this is to have you do a little exercise. Hold your arms straight out, have someone push sideways, and try to resist. Then repeat with your upper arms at your side and just your lower arms out. It is much easier to resist and your arms will not tire as fast.

Never "spoke" the wheel (hanging onto the steering wheel spokes) and do not hang onto the bottom, as this magnifies your hand movements and you have less leverage in an emergency. Never palm the wheel (spinning the wheel with an open hand) as you have no grip on the wheel, which means no positive control.

At this point let's talk about some things I call **road push** and **wind push**. When driving down the road sometimes your coach seems as if it has a mind of its own. It will take off in a direction that you weren't planning to go. Many roads have ruts, worn by heavy traffic, that generally have a different track width than your coach. What happens is that, unless you are perfectly centered, one tire or the other will want to drop into the rut, pushing you around. Even your tow vehicle can push you around. If this happens try moving to one side of the lane to see if you can find an area where things are in balance.

Another thing that can make the coach move around is the wind. I don't know how to describe it, it is just a seat-of-the-pants feel. The body of a coach with air suspension will sometimes move around on the axels. If the coach starts wandering, you should begin looking at indicators such as trees, road conditions, etc., to see what is influencing the movement. If you are chasing the body of the coach you can find yourself wandering all over the road. The lesson here is that you need to learn to steer the wheels not the coach.

Reference Points

Another problem some people have is maintaining a straight course. In a car you have a hood in front of you to use as a sight, but in a motorhome you have very little in front of you.

If you have ever ridden a ferry or other boat with a short front end you will usually see a framework that sticks out in front of the helmsman. That is called a "jackstaff," and it gives the helmsman something to sight over, to see if he is turning off course. A boat does not have lines to follow, like you do in your motorhome.

It is not practical to install a jackstaff on the front of your motorhome, so you need to establish reference points. You probably already do this subconsciously. Without looking, can you tell me what those points are? When you go to the parking lot to establish your turn data, park with the driver's side of the coach on a long line and see where that line intersects the bottom of the windshield. If there is no specific reference point, mark that spot with a piece of tape or one of those clear dots used to mark dings in the windshield. Then, move the coach, putting the line on the passenger side, and mark the windshield the same way. This will give you your limits. These marks will give your subconscious some help to stay centered in your lane and maintain a straight course. You should also note where your windshield marks or any reference points you have established on the dash are when centered on an average-width roadway.

Note where the lines on the pavement intersect the dash.

An example of how beneficial this can be is when you are driving on a dark, rainy night, and you come to a narrow bridge where there is on coming traffic. Just set your marks, and go because you will not be able to see anything else.

You also can use your marks on a bright, sunny day when the sun reflects off the windshield and all you see is one side of the road to keep yourself on a safe path.

These reference points work fine when driving along straight or gently curving roads. Do you also remember off-tracking and that you actually steer from the rear? As you drive curvy, twisty roads, steering from the rear to keep your wheels on the road, observe where the center and fog lines are in relationship to your reference marks. (The fog line is the solid line on the right side of the road.) This becomes very helpful when driving at night.

Remember that you steer from the rear, so you must drive the front a lot further out than you think to keep the rear wheels on the road. Also remember that reference points will be different for each driver.

Mirror: Friend or Foe?

Be sure to look around your mirrors.

The motor coach mirrors play a critical part in driving; they are helpful, of course, but they also can be your enemy. Those big mirrors that give you a good view behind your vehicle also block a large portion of your view looking forward. You can easily lose people, bicycles, small cars, and telephone poles behind them. You need to make sure that you look around them when driving.

hown in these pictures my wife and I are totally blocked by the mirror and we are only standing about twenty feet away from the coach.

Transmissions

"D" is for dummies. Most people just put their transmission in Drive, and then just drive. That is not the best thing to do in a larger rig. When you come to that hill, shift down one or maybe two gears as you proceed up the grade, before you start to lose speed. How many gears you shift up or down will vary from rig to rig; just be sure to keep an eye on your RPMs. You will find that in most cases you will climb the hill without as much reduction in speed, and you will get better fuel economy.

I am sure that you have heard the old adage that you go down a hill in the same gear that you needed to go up the hill. You are much better using the engine as a brake rather than using your brakes alone. It is far safer going downhill at 15 to 20 mph in first gear and using your brakes sparingly, rather than 30 to 35 mph and using your brakes more often.

If your coach is equipped with a retarder, the transmission is acting as a brake by restricting the transmission fluid. If you have a transmission retarder be sure to watch your transmission temperature, as it can rise rapidly during use.

Another very important thing to do when shifting from forward to reverse, or the other way around, is to pause or shift into neutral between forward and reverse to allow the drive train to relax before changing direction. With the new, more powerful engines in the diesel pushers, you can twist off a drive shaft very easily. The next picture is of a transmission output shaft from a coach with a 300-horsepower engine. The driver was still moving forward when he shifted into reverse. This shaft is only 1½" in diameter and costs $1200. It took two mechanics eight hours to replace the power unit. I'm sure that most of you do not have a spare power unit sitting in your garage.

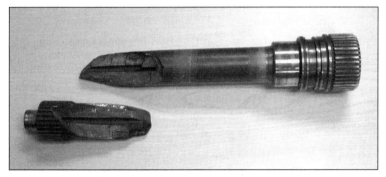

A twisted shaft. What you don't want to do.

Advisory Signs

When driving you see many advisory signs. In your car you may or may not slow down as much as the sign advises. When driving a large vehicle, however, slow down to the posted advisory speed, unless you have firsthand knowledge of the situation. It is always better to err on the side of caution.

Merging

Merging and lane changes can be a challenge sometimes. A larger vehicle cannot accelerate or decelerate as quickly as the general traffic. You need to maintain as much speed as possible when merging or changing lanes. Here is where I will teach you the use of **polite intimidation** and what the **cost coefficient** is.

In normal driving you just wait for a large enough space, turn your turn signal on, and move over. It is when traffic gets heavy that you need to get a little bit more creative. Don't just turn your signal on and wait for an opening. If you do that, most of the time no one will let you in, and after a while people will ignore your signal.

When you need to make your move, first move over to the opposite side of your lane from the direction you want to go, and then turn your signal on and move over quickly enough that the move is noticeable. When you move away first, it gives you more room to make your move more noticeable. The key here is to move over, but do not cross the line. As long as you stay in your lane, and don't cross the line out of your lane, you haven't violated anything. The movement generally will cause other drivers to back off, which opens a space for you to move into. If it doesn't work, turn off your signal, wait a while, and then try again. Just remember to move back over.

As a last resort you can use the cost coefficient. This is where, using your mirrors, you pick the most expensive car in the line of traffic coming up from behind. Turn your signal on just as the selected vehicle reaches your rear corner and can still see your turn signal, and then make your side movement. This works best if you have signals on the side of the coach. And don't forget to thank the person who let you in. You can blink your lights or turn your flashers on for two to three cycles.

Downtown

Let's talk a little about driving in town. I know what you are thinking, I don't drive downtown. Have you ever taken a wrong turn? You are reading this to yourself, so you can admit it.

Downtown streets are usually narrower than highways. In some cases the lanes are only eight feet wide. If you are driving an eight-and-a-half-foot wide coach you need to be very careful. If traffic is light, then just drive in your lane. If traffic is heavy it is sometimes better to straddle two lanes to be safe.

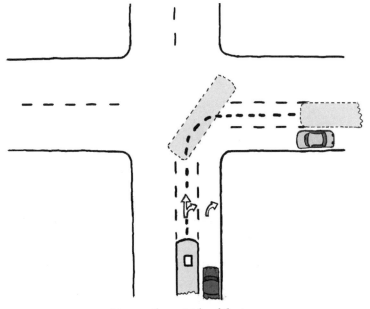

Stay on the outside of the turn.

Turning in town is harder to explain than it is to understand. In general it is best to be in the outer lane of the turn, the lane with the largest radius, when making turns on multiple-lane roads. When driving in big cities things change a little. The radius of the turn lanes is much smaller than your coach will turn. If there are double turn lanes, turn from the lane on the outside of the turn. Don't confuse the outer lane of the turn with the outside lane, which is the curb lane.

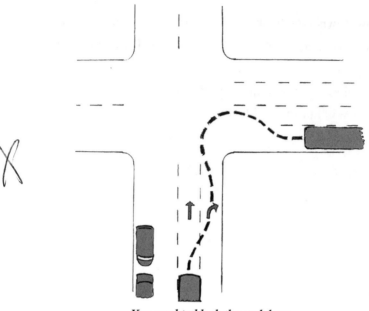

You need to block the curb lane.

If there is only a single turn lane you may have to do what is called a **buttonhook** turn. This is accomplished by setting up in the curb lane to block traffic from coming up alongside. When traffic is clear you would first turn to the opposite direction, leaving your tail in the curb lane, until you reach the point that you want to start your turn into the lane.

Don't forget to check your side mirrors during the turn. You should, at a minimum, check both sides at the start, middle, and end of the turn so you don't get surprised by cars or people who don't have any idea how much room it takes you to turn. Because if there is a space, other vehicles, especially cabs, will fill it. You should also be checking your tail swing. Remember that when you are turning left you have much better visibility to your inside than you do on a right turn.

Don't force a turn, wait for traffic to clear.

Backing

Backing a large vehicle can be a challenge. Even with a backup camera the view is somewhat distorted and takes some practice. The best way to back up is to have a spotter guide you. You need to be able to communicate by either hand signals or use radios. Talk first so you understand the signals. If you use hand signals make big movements and have the spotter stand where they can be seen in the mirror. This means that the spotter may need to move as you turn. You should always be able to see each other's face. If something doesn't look right, *stop*, get out and look. If you need to back up without any help walk the area first. Establish predetermined stop points, and then stop, check when you reach that predetermined point, and repeat this process as many time as needed. Before you start backing up tap your electric horn, not the air, to warn people around you.

The Parking Lot

Parking lots are an area where I see a lot of potential problems. One of the first things to be aware of is that the lane markings are not laid out for larger vehicles; in fact sometimes I don't think they are even laid out for cars. Disregard the markings and go by the obstructions that you need to avoid. When parking your rig find a place where you will not need to back up and where you cannot get blocked in. You need to park at the end of an angled row pointing out, or diagonally across spaces at the end of the row pointing out. What I mean by pointing out is pointing to the road out of the lot.

If the lot has straight-in parking, take as many spots as needed to ensure that you do not get blocked in. Always park at an angle.

Several times I have seen a driver pull into an empty lot and park as if they were parking a car. When they return after shopping they find cars parked all around them and are not able to get out. It may look fine when there is no one around. But, as you know, when you park your new car in the far corner of a lot so no one will ding a door, someone parks so close to you that you can't even get in when you return to the parking lot.

Adverse Weather

Adverse-weather driving is something that you will not normally be exposed to when driving your motorhome, unless you are a skier or a snowbird caught in an early or late winter storm. I am not going into a full-blown "How to drive in the snow" lesson, because it is basically the same as driving any other vehicle, but I will give you some things to think about.

After driving for awhile on snow or ice your tires will be warm when you stop. What can happen is that your warm tires will melt the surface ice, and if you are on a slope, your coach can start to slide. Even if you are on the flat, the tires will melt a depression so that when you want to move again all your wheels will do is spin in the depression, or if you waited too long, your tires can freeze to the ground. If your tires freeze to the ground, *don't try to overpower them to get them free.* This can lead to twisted or broken drive lines.

What I recommend is that you carry a bucket of dry sand. Why dry sand, you ask? Wet sand will freeze in the bucket and make it very hard to use. Can you spell "Sand-sickle"? After you stop, throw some sand in front of each wheel, and then move onto those sanded areas. Repeat the process in about an hour if possible.

Some bus companies don't require their drivers to sand and a few years back a non-sanded coach started to slide, and like dominos there was an entire line of coaches that slid together.

Another use for the sand is when trying to hold your coach on an icy hill. When you have your foot on your service brakes you are holding with all wheels; but when you set the parking brake and take your foot off the service brake, you are only holding with the rear wheels. Because of the weight and length of your coach the front end can start to slide. Make sure that your coach is staying put before you leave the driver's seat. As soon as you stop, throw some sand around the front wheels. This will help them stay put. Trust me, during the winter I drive ski charters so I get to play with coaches in the snow, and you don't want the front to start sliding when you are installing chains.

Dry your brakes before you stop for a long time. Use slight pedal pressure for about a mile, so they will warm up and dry out and they won't freeze.

Don't use your engine brake or retarder when the roads are slick. They can cause the rear wheels to break loose and send you into a skid.

---

*Drive smart: Proper planning
prevents poor performance.*

CHAPTER 4

The Art of Braking

"Whoa, Betsy!"

The braking technique that I teach motor coach drivers is **feather braking**. To feather-brake you apply the brakes gently, come down on them firmly, and then slowly back off the pedal as you come to a stop. This will take the "jerk" out of the end of the stop. When done correctly you can even make a panic stop as smooth as silk.

Don't forget to supplement your stopping power by using an auxiliary braking system if you have one. There are three basic types of auxiliary braking systems: compression brakes, most commonly called a jake brake; exhaust brakes, which are engine brakes that work off the exhaust back pressure; and a transmission retarder. Also use the transmission by shifting down. When driving in heavy traffic it is a good idea to keep your auxiliary braking system on to give you that extra edge.

Learn how to use your auxiliary braking system. Many people tell me that when they turn on their auxiliary braking system, their coach starts shifting down and coming to a stop. If this is happening to you, the coach is driving you, you are not driving the coach. There is a definite point between acceleration and deceleration. With every vehicle that I have driven I have been able to find that point where you are not accelerating or decelerating. I call that point **floating the throttle**.

There are two types of braking systems, hydraulic and air. If your coach is equipped with hydraulic brakes it operates basically the same as your car, but if you have air brakes there are a few more things that you need to know. You need to be familiar with some of the parts of the system and the operating pressures.

Air Brake Systems

At this point I need to add this note. When I talk about coach systems I am talking in general terms. I highly recommend that you do some research on your coach to see what you have.

An air brake system has the following basic parts:

The **air compressor** is used to maintain pressure for the braking system and the suspension. The air compressor governor should cut in when the pressure drops to about 100 psi. and should cut off at 125 psi.

The **foot brake**, which is also called the service brake, is a valve that operates the brakes. Every time you apply the foot brake you are pressurizing the brake system. Pushing the pedal down harder applies more pressure. Letting up on the brake pedal reduces the air pressure and releases the brakes. Releasing the brakes lets some compressed air go out of the system, so the air pressure in the air tanks is reduced. Pressing and releasing the brake pedal unnecessarily can let the air out faster than the compressor can replace it. The normal operating range for air brakes is 90 to 120 psi, but a good rule of thumb is that you should never start moving with less than 100 psi. If the system pressure drops below 90 psi, you may not have full brake efficiency.

The **parking brake** is that diamond-shaped yellow knob that you push to release the brakes and pull to set the brakes when parking.

Ensure that when you leave the driver's seat you have the parking brake set and the transmission in neutral. Coaches with an air brake system usually do not have a Park position on the transmission.

The **warning buzzer** should sound when the air pressure drops below 60 psi. On some vehicles it may sound as soon as 80 to 85 psi. There also may be a red light. If you hear the warning buzzer while driving, pull over immediately in a safe area and stop. Apply the brakes once and come to a stop. Do not pump the brakes because each time you push on the pedal you use up your air supply faster. It is much better to make a controlled stop, rather than having the emergency brake engage because if it does, that is where you stay. When building air pressure the buzzer may not go off until 80 to 85 psi.

The **emergency brake** system is a spring-loaded brake that will come on automatically when the air pressure drops to a range of 20 to 45 psi. The emergency brake system is very confusing to most people. They think it is similar to the emergency brake in their car. It is a separate system from the parking brake that only engages the brakes when the air pressure drops below the limit.

The **air storage tank** holds a sufficient quantity of compressed air to operate safely. Some systems have multiple tanks, one for each axle, and sometimes a third for the suspension.

The **pressure gauge** will indicate how much air you have in the storage tank(s). Some vehicles have two gages, and others have a single gage with two needles. You need to become familiar with the pressure gage(s).

The Braking Equation

When stopping a vehicle there are four phases that make up the stopping equation. These phases are:

1. **Perception time**, the time it takes to recognize that you need to stop.

2. **Reaction time**, the time it takes for you to apply the brakes.

3. **Brake lag**, the time from when you apply pressure on the pedal to when the brakes start to engage. For hydraulic systems the time is negligible, but for air systems it can be up to a half-second.

4. **Stopping distance**, the distance you travel after the brakes have engaged.

Out of those four phases, you have control over only one phase. Your reaction time is your reaction time, not much you can do to improve it. Brake lag for air brakes can be up to a half-second or more, it varies with vehicles and different types of braking systems, nothing you can do here either. Stopping distance is also a constant, your only control here is maintaining good tires and brakes. That leaves perception time, which is something you do have control over.

Braking Scenarios

- ## Scenario #1

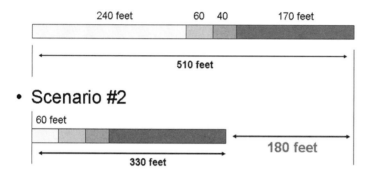

- ## Scenario #2

Let me lay out a couple of scenarios. If you are traveling 55 mph, which is about 80 feet per second, it takes you three seconds to perceive a problem. You have traveled about 240 feet before you start to react.

Your reaction time, about three-fourths of a second, will take you another 60 feet. So far you have traveled 300 feet. Brake lag can add up to another 40 feet. You are up to 340 feet, and you haven't started to stop yet. That's more than the length of a football field. With a nominal stopping distance of 170 feet you will have traveled a total of 510 feet before you have completed your stop.

Okay, now let's look at the same scenario using the perception time of a trained driver. The perception time for a trained driver is about three-fourths of a second, which means the driver would only travel 60 feet before starting to react. That is 180 feet less, which means you will stop 180 feet sooner.

Stop and think about that for a moment, 180 feet is over half the length of a football field. This would mean that you would stop in 330 feet versus 510 feet. I can lay out all sorts of scenarios, but three to five seconds' perception time is not unrealistic for the untrained driver.

Drive smart: Brake smartly.

CHAPTER 5

Mind Set

"Driving is 10 percent physical, 90 percent mental."

So what can you do to improve your perception time? Here is where I am going to introduce you to **perception driving** and the **principles of smart driving**, sometimes called "space cushion driving."

The National Safety Council reports that an average of one out of every four drivers is involved in a reportable accident every year. Tire marks at the scenes indicate that the trouble was seen, but often too late. In most cases the driver had robbed himself or herself of sufficient space or time to react to the hazard by following too closely. The closer you follow the more you focus on the vehicle in front of you. It is like wearing blinders and you don't see what is developing around you.

Perception Driving

To drive safely you perceive, predict, and perform. You must first perceive the potential trouble. This means seeing the hazard both physically (10 percent), and then understanding what it means, mentally (90 percent), to the driving situation. Only then can you predict what action is necessary in order to avoid being involved in a collision. Then you must perform such action in time, before it is too late.

The Principles of Smart Driving

Okay, how do you do it? You learn to use the following principles.

• **Aim high in steering.** While driving, your main consideration is to find a safe path for your vehicle to travel. You do the same basic thing for any activity. When you walk for example, at 3 to 4 mph, you look about 25 feet ahead, and your stopping distance is about 2 feet. As the speeds increase the distance you need to be aware of increases many times over. Set your sights high. When driving in the city, look at least one block ahead, and on the highway look at least a quarter of a mile ahead. A rule of thumb is to set your sights to where you will be in about fifteen seconds. At first try counting this out just like following distance. You will be surprised at how your eye can deceive you when it comes to measuring distance, especially at highway speeds.

If you are not looking far enough ahead you are **low aim sighting**. Some indications of low aim sighting are:

1. Hugging one side of the road.
2. Swinging wide to avoid parked vehicles.
3. Over steering on turns, making wide unnecessary sweeps.
4. Swinging the opposite direction before making a turn.

These actions indicate that your eyes are leading your wheels.

You also need to be careful not to establish a fixed stare straight ahead, which leads me to the next principle.

• **Get the big picture.** What is the big picture? Your traffic picture is the sum total of every conflict that can be perceived. It is not only what you see, but what you should see. Remember this is a constantly changing picture. Earlier I talked about aiming high and now you need to expand that. In town look at least one block ahead and sidewalk to sidewalk. On the highway look ahead at least one-fourth mile and fence to fence. Don't forget to include what is behind you. Remember, 30 percent of the hazards come from the rear. Your big picture should contain stationary objects, such as traffic lights and signs, lamp poles, parked vehicles, and obstructions, as well as moving objects such as people in vehicles, people walking, bicycles, and motorcycles. Basically, anything that can move may become a hazard. You also need to observe instructions, warnings, and traffic control devices. Being aware of all these things gives you an opportunity to anticipate the actions of others.

• **Keep your eyes moving.** The only way you can satisfactorily perform the first two principles is to keep your eyes moving. Your big picture is constantly changing so you continually need to scan the surrounding area and your mirrors to update your data input. You should make a complete scanning cycle about every eight seconds, even when you are stopped.

Okay, now that I have told you where to look, how to look, and what to look for, what do you do with that information? Your eyes are only part of this equation, you need to use your mind to interpret the data. If you look at a picture you may not see the subtle details. As you keep your eyes moving you need to identify each potential hazard, what the hazard may do, and what your response should be. An example of an individual hazard would be a car on a crossroad coming to a stop sign. Is the car slowing down or is it coming too fast? Do you do nothing, slow down, stop, or take evasive action? As you identify each hazard prioritize them in the order you need to address them.

At first this seems like too much to do, but after a while you can do it subconsciously. I start my students out by asking them to tell me what they see and what the potential hazard is. There is no way you can say out loud what your mind is thinking, but this is a good exercise to get the thought process started. Most of this you are already doing, you just need to refine it and adjust it to a larger vehicle.

• **Leave yourself an out.** The first thing you need to do in leaving yourself an out is maintain a safe following distance. With all that data I have just told you to gather and evaluate you need some time and space to do something with it. I am sure that you all remember the two-second rule, or one car length for every ten mph following distance that you were taught when you learned to drive. Well, that is fine for a car, not an RV. The larger the vehicle, the more distance you need.

The basic rule of thumb for following distance is one second for every ten feet of vehicle length for speeds up to 40 mph, and add one second for speeds over 40 mph. I would recommend that if you are over a ten-foot increment round up to the next break. If you have a tow, include the tow in the length. The following distance times are based on having brakes on all wheels, including what you are towing. Using this rule the recommended minimum following distance for a forty-foot overall length would be four seconds on dry payment for speeds up to 40 mph. For speeds 40 mph and above, this would be expanded to five seconds. These

7 Sec.

times should be further expanded to suit conditions such as wet payment, mud, or snow and ice. Adding an additional second for each is not unreasonable. These distances are for speeds over 40 mph, so you need to add a second to each. I know what you are thinking, there is no way I can maintain that much following distance. I agree, you probably won't be able to maintain the proper following distance all the time, but try your best. You might be surprised how often you can maintain the proper distance. Maintaining a safe following distance will give you time and room to maneuver to avoid hazards. To measure following distance note when the vehicle ahead of you passes a mark on the road then start counting, one thousand and one, one thousand and two, etc., until you reach that mark. In addition, don't let your cruise control set you up by getting you too close behind someone.

You also need to leave yourself an out when stopped. A rule of thumb is to stop so you can see the rear wheels of the vehicle ahead of you. This will give you sufficient room to maneuver if traffic stalls. Also, when going through an intersection, check to be sure there is enough room for your entire rig to clear the intersection when you stop. Don't forget your towed vehicle. This sometimes can be very hard because people will drive around you and fill the hole, but if you pull up and do not clear the intersection, you will get the ticket, not them.

• **Make sure they see you.** Drive with your lights on. When approaching a potential conflict, make eye contact if possible. Observe the driver. Is the driver looking at you? Is there a blank look on the person's face? Is the driver looking around as if searching for an address? Is the vehicle traveling faster than the rest of the traffic, and is there a place for it to go into? Can you even see in the other car's window? You may need to flash your lights, or gently honk your horn. It is better to try to make contact early than waiting till the last second when you lose your time and space to maneuver. Waiting too long may even cause the incident.

• **Always be prepared to yield.** Even though you may have done everything correctly, others may not. Even if you do make eye contact with the other person and you have the legal right of way, the driver may not give it to you. A good example of this is when cars merge on the freeway. Instead of yielding they think that if they have their turn signal on, if used, that they have the right of way. Another area that is a challenge is intersections. When approaching an intersection watch the light. When did it change last? If it was green when you first saw it, consider it a stale green light. Look for things like the pedestrian crossing lights and cars creeping into the intersection. You need to proceed with caution. You may even want to lift your foot off the accelerator and cover the brake, which will reduce your overall stopping distance. When driving along a street, watch the vehicles parked alongside the street. If they just pulled in, you can bet they will open their door in front of you. Watch for the exhaust that would indicate a running engine or the telltale signs of taillights coming on, as if the driver is putting it in gear to get ready to pull out. Expect the unexpected. Be proactive not reactive.

• **Drive in a manner in which you control the outcome.** And now we have come to the last of the principles. None of the previous principles are any good if you do not have the right attitude. Do a "Check up from the Neck up." As I said earlier, you need to perceive, predict, and perform. If your mind is not in the right state, you become reactive and you let others control you. Be cautious about others yet confident in your abilities. In other words be proactive not reactive.

Learn to accept what the other driver will do. It works against you if you get upset. Maintain your composure and you will control the outcome.

Drive smart: Keep your head in the game.

CHAPTER 6

Homework

"You thought you could get out of this easily, didn't you."

I have now given you all the attributes that you need to learn and master; so how do you master them? Here is where you get a homework assignment. The best way we have found is to think out loud when driving. Your brain works much faster than your mouth, but you need to start somewhere. Start by describing what you see and where you see it. Then, evaluate what the potential hazards are, and figure out your course(s) of action. I would suggest doing this while you are driving by yourself, otherwise it will drive your passenger nuts.

Practice shuffle steering, feather braking, and smart driving.

I have created a data worksheet and placed it in the appendix for you to record your turning information along with some other useful data. Do not forget to record the measurements in meters also. This could become very handy if you go to Canada or Mexico.

I also like to know the weight by wheel, which is helpful for proper loading and tire inflation. You can go to a public scale or stop at a weigh station along the highway when it is closed. Most will have the scale readout visible or a remote readout you can see.

Drive smart.

(Write this one hundred times on the blackboard.)

Sorry, I just had to say it.

CHAPTER 7

Closing

I encourage you to seriously study, practice, and attain the confidence to become a professional driver.

My main objective in writing this book is to provide you with tools to help you have better control of your motorhome and become a safer driver, just like a professional. But I will confess that many of the techniques I have covered are also designed for passenger comfort. I know what you're thinking—"I don't carry passengers like a bus driver." *Well, remember you usually have a passenger, and if you make them uncomfortable it can make for some cold nights.*

---

*Drive smart: Enjoy the journey by driving
your motorhome like a pro!*

Data Worksheet

Height:

    Hard   _____ ft / _____ m

    Soft   _____ ft / _____ m

    Width   _____ ft/ _____ m

Weight:

	Front	**Rear**		
Right	_____	_____		
Left	_____	_____		
Total	_____	_____ =	_____lb/	_____kg

    Tail swing_____

Turn offsets:

    @ 1 foot _____

    @ 2 feet _____

    @ 3 feet _____

    @ 4 feet _____

    @ 5 feet _____

    @ 6 feet _____

ORDER PAGE

For additional copies, please send your check or
money order for $12.95 including shipping to:

Drive Smart
PO Box 3690
Silverdale, WA 98383-3690

DRIVERS LICENSE

WALSH, LORRIN
PO BOX 3690
SILVERDALE, WA 98383

CDL

Lorrin Walsh first got involved with RVs in the early sixties when his parent bought a 13-foot camp trailer. Later he bought a trailer of his own, and then traded it for a motorhome in 1975. He and his wife are on their fifth motorhome.

A few years ago, after retirement from his job as a quality assurance inspector, Lorrin went to work for Gray Line of Seattle® as a driver/guide, just for fun. He became an instructor and currently works for them and their parent company, Holland America Line®, where he just finished a six-month promotional trip on the East Coast driving a 45-foot motor coach.